IT'S SCIENCE!

he Five Senses

Sally Hewitt

CHILDREN'S PRESS®

A Division of Grolier Publishing
NEW YORK • LONDON • HONG KONG • SYDNEY
DANBURY, CONNECTICUT

Acknowledgments:
Ardea pp. 25tl (Adrian Warren), 27l (John Daniels); Bruce Coleman
pp. 11b (William S. Paton), 19b (Michael Fogden), 23t (Stephen J.
Krasemann), 25tm (Dr. Frieder Sauer); Frank Lane Picture Agency pp.
9b (Gerard Lacz), 11tl (Mark Newman), 11tr (W. Wisniewski); Getty
Images p. 26r (Pascal Crapet); Robert Harding pp. 14bl (Flip Nicklin);
Natural History Photography Agency pp. 21 (Stephen Dalton),
22r (A.N.T./Kelvin Aitken), 25b (Daniel Heuclin); Oxford Scientific Films
pp. 18r (Roger Jackman), 19t (G.A. Maclean), 23b (Tom Ulrich), 25tr
(Bob Fredrick); Planet Earth Pictures pp. 13t (Neil McIntyre); Shout
Picture Library p. 22l; Stock Market pp. 9tl, 9tr, 14br, 15t.

Series editor: Rachel Cooke
Designer: Mo Choy
Picture research: Alex Young
Photography: Ray Moller unless otherwise acknowledged
Series consultant: Sally Nankivell-Aston

First published in 1998 by Franklin Watts
First American edition 1999 by Children's Press
A Division of Grolier Publishing
90 Sherman Turnpike
Danbury, CT 06816

Visit Children's Press on the Internet at:
http://publishing.grolier.com

Library of Congress Cataloging-in-Publication Data
Hewitt, Sally.
    The five senses / Sally Hewitt.
        p. cm.
    Includes index.
    Summary: Examines the fives senses possessed by humans, how
they are used, and how they compare to those of animals.
    ISBN 0-516-21179-X (lib. bdg.) 0-516-26447-8 (pbk.)
    1. Senses and sensation--Juvenile literature. [1. Senses and
sensation.] I. Title.
QP434.H49 1999
573.8'7--dc21
                                                                98-15042
                                                                    CIP
                                                                     AC

GROLIER
PUBLISHING

Contents

The Five Senses

Your five **senses** tell you what is going on around you. Do you know what they are?

When Jack eats an orange, he uses all his five senses.

He sees the shape and color of the orange.

He hears the munching sound he makes as he chews.

He feels the shape of the orange and the roughness of its skin.

He can smell the orange.

He can taste its sweet juice.

TRY IT OUT!

Eat a piece of fruit that you like.
Use all your senses!
What can you see, hear, feel, smell, and taste?

Different parts of your body send messages to your **brain** so that you can understand what you are seeing, hearing, feeling, smelling, and tasting.

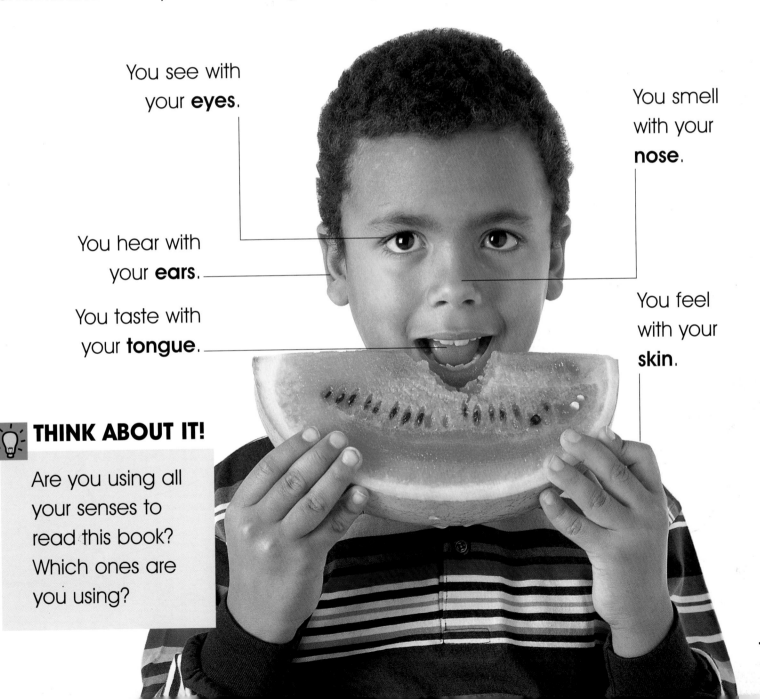

You see with your **eyes**.

You smell with your **nose**.

You hear with your **ears**.

You taste with your **tongue**.

You feel with your **skin**.

💡 **THINK ABOUT IT!**

Are you using all your senses to read this book? Which ones are you using?

Seeing

You see when you open your eyes and let light into them. What can you see when you shut your eyes and keep out the light?

You see colors, shapes, and things moving with your eyes.

What shapes and colors can you see in this picture? Is there something you have never seen before?

You can only look at the things in this picture. When you find something new, you might have to touch it, listen to it, or smell it to find out exactly what it is.

TRY IT OUT!

Choose one of the things you can see in the picture. Try drawing and coloring it. Be careful to copy the color and shape.

These two pictures are of the same place, but one was taken in daylight and the other when it was getting dark. Which one is the most colorful?

Your eyes can only see color well in the light.

Animals that go out at night see much better in the dark than we do, but their eyes cannot see color very well. A cat sees things mostly in black and white.

TRY IT OUT!

Shut the curtain in your bedroom in the daytime, but let in a crack of light. How much color can you see?
Now open the curtains. How much color can you see now?

Two Eyes

Having two eyes at the front of your head helps you figure out exactly how near or how far away things are.

TRY IT OUT!

Hold a pen out in front of you in one hand and the cap in the other hand. Shut one eye and try putting the cap on the pen. Now open both eyes and try again. Is it easier with one eye open or two?

Hunters, such as leopards, have both eyes in the front of their heads like us. They need to be able to figure out exactly where their **prey** is.

This antelope might be a leopard's next meal. Its eyes are on the sides of its head, which means it can see all around. It will quickly spot an **enemy** such as a leopard and try to run away—before it is too late!

 THINK ABOUT IT!

This bird's eyes are on the sides of its head. What animals might it be watching out for? When you look at pictures of animals, notice the size, shape, and location of their eyes and think about why they are like that.

Hearing

The sounds you hear with your ears can give you a lot of **information** about things you may not be able to see.
Imagine the sounds that are made by spinning a coin, stirring tea, cutting paper, and running a finger along a comb.

 **TRY IT OUT!**

Get some friends to shut their eyes while you make some sounds like the ones in the picture. Ask them to tell you what they are hearing.

Many animals use their sense of hearing to help keep them safe. A rabbit pricks up its ears and listens for danger. It warns the other rabbits to run for cover by thumping its back leg on the ground.

All kinds of animals prick up their ears to hear better.

You cannot prick up your ears like a rabbit, but try cupping your ears toward a sound such as a radio playing softly. It makes a sound easier to hear.

👁 LOOK AGAIN

Look again at page 11 for an animal that has eyes on the sides of its head and ears to hear all around that help tell it that an enemy is nearby.

13

Listen To This!

One of the most important ways we use our sense of hearing is to listen to what people are saying. You might listen to a story being read to you or your teacher telling you something new. Sometimes you might just enjoy chatting.

THINK ABOUT IT!

Can you remember any of the things that have been said to you today? Were any of them important messages?

Animals use sounds to send messages to each other, too.

Whales sing out strange noises to each other underwater.

Lambs bleat when they need to find their mothers. Their mothers call "baa!" back.

14

You can use your eyes as well as your ears to figure out what people are telling you.

People who cannot hear use their eyes instead of their ears to understand what people are saying to them. They use **sign language** and can tell what people are saying by watching their lips move.

 TRY IT OUT!

Without making a sound, try asking a friend to come to your house to play. Now tell your friend silently that you are hungry and want something to eat.

THINK ABOUT IT!

When you listen to someone speaking to you, where do you look? Do you understand better if you look at the person speaking to you?

15

Touch

You can tell a lot about something just by touching it. When you touch something, you feel what it is like. Imagine feeling the hairbrush in this picture with your eyes shut. You would quickly guess what it was because you have seen and felt a hairbrush before.

 **TRY IT OUT!**

Ask a friend to put some objects into a pillowcase, including something that you have never seen before. Make sure that there are no sharp edges or points. Try to guess what the objects are just by feeling them. Which ones are easy to guess and which ones are difficult?

Your skin is the part of your body that you feel with. The skin on your fingertips is very **sensitive** to touch, so they are very good for feeling things.

 TRY IT OUT!

Ask a friend to shut her eyes. Touch both points of a hairpin on the back of her hand. How many points can she feel? Touch the points on her fingertips. How many points can she feel now? Which is more sensitive, the skin on her fingertips or the skin on the back of her hands?

LOOK AGAIN

Look again at page 6. What does Jack feel with his fingers?

17

Feelers

Animals feel things with their skin as you do, but they have other ways of feeling things, too.

Have you ever played blindman's-buff or put out your hands to feel what is around you to stop yourself from bumping into something in the dark?

Mice's **whiskers** work in the same way. They help mice feel what is going on all around them in the dark.

 **LOOK AGAIN**

Look again at page 9. How do you think the cat's whiskers help it hunt?

Snails have feelers on top of their heads called **antennae**. The antennae reach out and feel if something is in the way before the snail bumps into it.

Insects have amazing antennae, which they use to touch and feel things. They also use their antennae to smell, taste, and hear!

THINK ABOUT IT!

How many other animals can you think of that have whiskers or antennae?
Why do you think antennae are sometimes called feelers?

19

Smell

You can't see smells, but they are all around you in the air you breathe. The part of your body that senses smell is right up inside your nose—so you smell better if you give a good sniff!

Most things have some kind of smell. Have you smelled any of these before?

Flowers smell sweet.

Your favorite food smells delicious.

A dirty dishcloth smells disgusting.

TRY IT OUT!

Ask an adult to help you choose some things with a strong smell, such as a lemon, some soap, or a shoe. See if a friend can guess what the objects are without seeing or touching them—just by sniffing.
Don't sniff powders like flour or talc, as they can get up your nose and damage it.

Smells often give important messages.

The sweet smell of a flower tells a bee that there is food to eat.

Fresh food smells good and makes you feel hungry and ready to eat.

The bad smell of a dirty dishcloth warns you that it is full of **germs**. You know it is time to find a clean one.

Sniffing Out

Many animals have a powerful sense of smell. They learn much more about what is going on around them through smell than people do.

The police use dogs to help them find things by sniffing.

There are smells in the water as well as in the air. Sharks can sniff out blood in the water from a long way away.

👁 LOOK AGAIN

Look again at page 11. The leopard can hunt its prey by smell before it even sees it. How does the antelope use its sense of smell?

Animals often have a strong **scent** so that they can smell each other.

It is easy for a baby deer to be separated from its mother in a big herd. The mother knows which one is her baby by its smell.

A fox marks out the area it lives and hunts in with a strong smell that warns other foxes to keep away!

TRY IT OUT!

How good is your sense of smell? Peel an orange and put it on a plate. Ask a friend to hide it in a room. Can you find the orange just by using your sense of smell?

Taste

Stick out your tongue and look at it in the mirror. Can you see little bumps on it? These are your **taste buds**. Your taste buds can taste things that are salty, sweet, sour, or bitter. What do the foods and drinks in this picture taste like— salty, sweet, sour, or bitter?

Sometimes you can tell what's for dinner just by the smell. The food's smell adds to its taste.

Have you noticed that food doesn't have such a strong taste when you have a cold and can't smell very well?

TRY IT OUT!

Hold your nose and shut your eyes while you eat a piece of apple, then bread, then banana, and then cheese. Can you tell what you are eating just by the taste? Now try without holding your nose. Can you taste them better?

Animals use their sense of taste a lot as well. This chimpanzee is feasting on sweet tasting fruit.

This caterpillar is poisonous and has a nasty taste. A bird who has pecked it once learns never to eat this kind of caterpillar again.

Flying insects can taste with their feet! They know at once whether they have landed on something good to eat.

THINK ABOUT IT!

What food do you like to taste? Do you like the smell as well? Can you think of some food that you like to taste but you don't like to smell?

Snakes flicker their tongues and taste the air. This way they can tell if there is food or danger nearby.

25

Keeping Safe

Animals keep alert and use their senses all the time to warn them of danger. You use your five senses to look out for danger signals, too. You learn and remember them, and this helps keep you safe.

You have been told to "stop, look, and listen!" when you cross a road. You look both ways for traffic, and you listen for the sound of cars as well, before you decide if it is safe to cross.

 **LOOK AGAIN**

> Look again at page 21. What danger signal does a bad smell give you?

Your skin feels hot when you get too close to a radiator. You know not to touch it because it could burn you.

Food that has rotted usually smells bad. You know it is not good to eat it. The food would probably taste nasty, too. What do you think you might do if you had a mouthful?

THINK ABOUT IT!

Look at this cat. It is using its senses to find out if it has found something to eat, to play with, or to be very careful of!

When you go somewhere new or see something strange, think about how you are using your senses to find out about what is going on around you.

27

Useful Words

Antennae Some animals, such as snails and insects, have long, sensitive feelers on their heads called antennae. Antennae can be used to touch, smell, taste, or hear.

Brain Your brain is inside your head. You think with your brain and use it to make sense of the world around you.

Ears Ears are the part of your body that you hear with. The ear flaps on the sides of your head collect sound. Inside your head are the parts of the ear that are sensitive to sound.

Enemy An enemy is someone who may do you harm. Animals that hunt are enemies of the animals they eat.

Eyes Your eyes are the part of your body that you see with. They are sensitive to light and color.

Germs Germs carry diseases that can make you feel sick. Germs are too tiny to see.

Hunter Hunters are animals that catch and kill other animals for food.

Information Information is anything you can know. Information can be the facts you see on the television news. Your senses give you information about what is happening around you.

Nose Your nose is sensitive to smells in the air. You smell things when you breathe in through your nose.

Prey Animals that are hunted and killed by other animals for food are called prey.

Scent A scent is a kind of smell. Many animals have a strong scent so that they can smell each other.

Senses Seeing, hearing, feeling, smelling, and tasting are the five senses. You use your senses to tell you what is going on all around you.

Sensitive Being sensitive means to be able to sense things. The parts of your body that you sense with are sensitive in different ways. For example, your skin is sensitive to touch, and your nose is sensitive to smell.

Sign language People who cannot hear use sign language. They use hand signs and body movements instead of sounds to talk to communicate with each other.

Skin Your skin is the part of your body that you feel with. It is sensitive to touch.

Taste buds Taste buds are the little bumps on your tongue that are sensitive to taste. They tell you if food or drink is sweet, salty, sour, or bitter.

Tongue Your tongue is inside your mouth. You taste with your tongue.

Whiskers Whiskers are long, sensitive hairs that grow around the mouths of many animals. They help the animal feel what is going on around them.

Index

About This Book

Children are natural scientists. They learn by touching and feeling, noticing, asking questions, and trying things out for themselves. The books in the *It's Science!* series are designed for the way children learn. Familiar objects are used as starting points for further learning. *The Five Senses* starts with a child eating an orange and explores how the senses work.

Each double-page spread introduces a new topic, such as hearing. Information is given, questions asked, and activities suggested that encourage children to make discoveries and develop new ideas for themselves. Look for these panels throughout the book:

TRY IT OUT! indicates a simple activity, using safe materials, that proves or explores a point.
THINK ABOUT IT! indicates a question inspired by the information on the page but points the reader to areas not covered by the book.
LOOK AGAIN introduces a cross-referencing activity that links themes and facts through the book.

Encourage children not to take the familiar world for granted. Point things out, ask questions, and enjoy making scientific discoveries together.